Praise for
chopping wood in the moonlight

When most of us retreated from the outside world in 2020, we had time to step back, to contemplate, to mourn, and to hope. Ken Letko's poems explore the range of this experience, filtering the external world through interior contemplation. From the candor of loneliness in "My Shield of Shadows": "…without/disappointments/some days I'd have/no appointments at all," to the celebration of a solitary moment in the forest, "the deer/become ferns/next to red alders," ("Bright Angel"), these poems encourage us to look deeper into our everyday experiences of the world, to move into a space of hopefulness, and breathe again.

—Kris Bigalk, Minneapolis, Minnesota

***

These lively, imaginative poems make for easy reading. Sometimes whimsical, sometimes profound, but always unpunctuated, they range in reference from Norman Rockwell to Carl Jung and celebrate what one poem's title calls "Mundane Excitement." Not all wood-choppers are connoisseurs of firewood, but Ken Letko is.

—Clemens Starck, Dallas, Oregon

***

Ken Letko's poetry occupies the cold places: the Wisconsin woods and California's Northern Coast. Reading Ken's words is a walk through nature reminiscent of Gary Snyder. At that same time, Ken's good humor and unconventional take on what he sees—a deer and an alder tree merge in one line of verse—make this accessible to readers no matter what the temperature is where they enjoy his poems.

—John Bell, Sacramento, California

chopping wood
in the
moonlight

chopping wood in the moonlight

poems by
Ken Letko

Flowstone Press
Illinois Valley, Oregon

Chopping Wood in the Moonlight
Copyright © 2021 Ken Letko

Front cover art *Lady of the Forest* © Denice Hart
used with permission

Back cover art *Red Mountain Crescent Moon* (2016) © Ken Letko

Back cover author photography by Denice Hart

First Flowstone Press Edition • May 2021
ISBN 978-1-945824-45-6

Flowstone Press,
an Imprint of Left Fork
www.leftforkbooks.com

Dedication

With gratitude for the spirit of the forest

—KL

Contents

How the Mountain Made Its Soul	3
Bright Angel	4
Enjoying Illusions	6
Slow Traveler	7
Turkey Vulture	8
Gravel	10
Making the Worst the Best	13
Cauliflower and the Brain	14
Belief	15
Some Reasons for Chopping Wood in the Moonlight	16
Beach Glass	18
Dear Norman Rockwell	19
Responding to the Internet	21
Transformation	22
Understanding Sports	23
A Few Rounds to Go	24
Dear Carl Jung	26
My Shield of Shadows	27
Mundane Excitement	28
History Flows	29
Push and Pull	30
Sparrow Grass	32
Standing Near a Whale Skull at Night	33
Acknowledgments	35
About the Author	36

chopping wood
in the
moonlight

How the Mountain Made Its Soul

the eternal secret
granite knows

as crystals cool
and learn to lie

still telling
the truth

forever

Bright Angel

gloaming is the time
of day when ferns
become deer

the night hawk
croaks at the bottom
of a dive into mosquitoes

in my memory suddenly
from the South Rim
I'm hiking the Bright Angel

make it to Indian Gardens
giant cottonwoods shade
the creek flowing strong

when I look up
the Milky Way
is a prayer

blanketing the Tonto

Plateau above

in the wavering heat

I camp on the flat

without a tent

the deer are so close

I can hear them chew

their evening browse

because I wander

in and out of sleep

daylight comes on

in my own meadow

and the deer

become ferns

next to red alders

Enjoying Illusions

I've left the little smudge
on the glass window

of the back door
because I like the way

it looks like a rabbit
running through the yard

when I turn my head
a certain way

the dead are finished
sleeping forever

that's why the turnover
rate is so low

how many windows
have you washed today?

Slow Traveler

the alder seed rides
in the belly of a quail

every sapling
is a pilgrimage

toward sunlight
wind a companion

that twists trunk
and limbs organically

without reason patience
is a slow traveler

Turkey Vulture

climbs over a mountain
without taking a step

enjoys leftovers
almost every day

though never invited
to Thanksgiving dinner

the turkey vulture
shares with coyotes

cats and wolves
and sometimes locates

a meal just by its smell
though closely related

to the stork the turkey vulture
does not deliver babies

but like the stork

the turkey vulture

goes bareheaded year round

tends to mate for life

and is an usher who helps

others on the journey

to the other side

Gravel

birthplace of salmon
steelhead and cutthroat

your crunch alerts me
to the approaching vehicle

in winter you provide
traction in summer

you help me enjoy
sandals and boots

you're the name
my old hiking friend

bestowed on trail mix
loosely mixed you're

ancient water filter
a few trowelfuls

in each geranium pot
bright pink in a plastic

bag you complete
my fish bowl kit

a piece of gravel
is a boulder to climb

and descend for an ant
a few pieces of the finest

in the grouse's crop
good for digestion

what passing a kidney
stone reminds me of

Tom Waits rasps
"Small Change"

misspelling of grovel
and gavel detour ahead

cousin to fresh oil
you're married to

Portland cement
Oregon to Maine

densely compacted
you support foundations

for so many buildings

Making the Worst the Best

look at the woodpile

choose the best piece

put it on the fire

let it burn down

look at the woodpile

choose the best piece

put it on the fire

let it burn down

look at the woodpile

choose the best piece

put it on the fire

let it burn down

Cauliflower and the Brain

each grows and matures
at a different rate

only experts can tell
males from females

the main stem strong
and growth silent

in the external world
both are cousins

to cabbage head
both lend shape

ideas to cumulus clouds
thunder into Parkinson's

syndrome and cauliflower
ear both can smell

a pot of water boiling

Belief

those lobster mushrooms
we picked along the trail

grew while we hiked
on the way back

they responded to our hope
we did not fail to see them

on the hike in

Some Reasons for Chopping Wood in the Moonlight   *for Li Po*

the rain let up at moonrise

and woodpiles never sleep

I didn't get enough chopped

during daylight hours

fishing has been so great

I enjoyed the river almost all week

chopping wood in sunlight

is too hot and sweaty

chopping wood without any

light is very difficult

as Li Po knew, the emperor's work

is never done and chopping wood

goes well with cold beer

or some red wine

I spent all of yesterday
writing poems

my muse often keeps me
lounging in the bath daylong

I need kindling every morning
and the owl shows me how

to glide through trees
when I sleep I listen to the ocean

and let the tides
make split decisions

Beach Glass

the ocean beach
burnishes a broken
beer bottle

the glass needs
a few decades
to sober up

enough to
remember
it is sand

Dear Norman Rockwell

when I was about twelve
or thirteen, Pusky,

owner of Leona's
Store, would give me

a Popsicle if I would
burn boxes in a fifty

gallon drum in the
alley he'd give me two

or three light anywhere
matches I'd carry

the boxes from the back
of the store set one ablaze

and as it crumbled and sparked
a rectangular metal grate

leaned against the barrel
I could place it on top

if I thought the ascending
glowing ash looked like trouble

or when I was done
and ready to go in

to get my Popsicle

Responding to the Internet

The Five Best States to Retire In
        the state of generosity
        the state of comfortable knowing
        the state of complete wealth
        the state of perfect weather
        the state of perpetual ecstasy

The Five Worst States to Retire In
        the state of greed
        the state of eternal doubt
        the state of complete poverty
        the state of unending storms
        the state of perpetual misery

Transformation

justice become just
ice without the right
space and memory

is all the planets
rotating around
the sun

yet when I take off
my glasses the evening
planets become stars

and an old dog
feels the thunder
coming

this is why
when a raven
enjoys sunshine

black becomes
purple

Understanding Sports

love means nothing

and deuce means equal

grand slam means tennis players

and baseball players eating

breakfast together at Denny's

a blooper lands just

beyond home plate

an artist's perspiration

dribbles in the paint

crossing the blue line

is not out of bounds

and unrestricted smoking

defines Bogey and red zone

portends hot possibilities

a field goal is not measured

in bushels of wheat

without notifying officials

the libero can join

the back row

to make a few digs

this is how I reduce

my handicap

A Few Rounds to Go

the child in a tantrum
clings to a painted pony

row row row
your boat

the golfer heads
into the playoffs

the patched up boxer
steps back into the ring

the wood splitter watches
the completed pile grow

Davey takes stock
at the Alamo

ninety-nine bottles
of beer on the wall

an hour before
closing time

what goes around

Dear Carl Jung

*I stand on my
darkness* I said
to my shadow

my shadow
did not call
me a liar

My Shield of Shadows

the evening arrives
slowly eats the light
the daytime shadows

that protected me
from the ultraviolet rays
have become my blanket

of warmth against
the cool moon
the darkest ache begins

to bend my shield
the worry that follows
me begins to step back

repelled by my shield
with surprise I begin
to see that without

disappointments
some days I'd have
no appointments at all

Mundane Excitement

accidently drop
my favorite coffee cup
but it doesn't break

an asparagus spear
pushes through soil

bring home
a new kitten

a skunk waddles
under the porch

bite through the skin
of a chilled grape

brush varnish
on a new shelf
and watch it dry

History Flows

even though I sleep warm
under an old wool blanket

my head is not covered
inside all slaves are set free

and I have a young daughter
who tends sheep in a meadow

this is how history flows
when a field mouse on the run

knows how to stay still
at just the right moment

bones don't like clutter
but they enjoy carrying

some muscle and a little fat

Push and Pull

fragile and tough
the spider web

loved and hated
the raindrop

vigilant though asleep
the watchdog

sugary but tart
red huckleberry pie

short-lived but eternal
the mosquito

energized but weary
the marathoner

slippery but sticky
the watermelon seed

hot and cold
a cup of tea

space and dust
everything

light and heavy
the human heart

life and death
all of us

Sparrow Grass

back when an avocado
was called alligator pear

mammoth wandered
the meteor shower

the fetid moss at each hoof step
developing earthen perfume

all prior life
all after life

in ultraviolet waves
a scorpion glows bright

the universe is light
and dust

asparagus is another way
to say sparrow grass

Standing Near a Whale Skull at Night

tonight as I look up through the plum
tree branches the crescent moon
sends quiet light onto the old
sun-bleached whale skull placed
near the young sapling
more than thirty years ago

memory is nearly strong enough
to conjure rotting whale flesh odor
which needed years to disappear

tonight as I look up through the plum
the newly formed fragrant blossoms
pulse on a flimsy wind
the darkness is so quiet
yet no matter how much I try
I cannot smell the moon

Acknowledgments

Thank you to the editors who supported publication of some of the poems included in this volume.

Askew. "Dear Carl Jung" and "Sparrow Grass."

Bohemian Renaissance. "Transformation, "A Few Rounds to Go," and "Mundane Excitement."

California Quarterly. "Responding to the Internet."

Lake Effect. "Enjoying Illusions."

Open: Journal of Arts & Letters. "Bright Angel."

Spillway. "Slow Traveler."

Turtle Island Quarterly. "Beach Glass."

About the Author

Originally from the Chequamegon Bay area of Northern Wisconsin, Ken Letko now lives in the redwoods of Del Norte, California's northernmost coastal county. He has taught writing at Bowling Green State University in Ohio, the Xian Foreign Languages Institute (now the Xian International Studies University) in the People's Republic of China, and College of the Redwoods in Crescent City, California. *Bright Darkness*, published by Flowstone Press in 2017, is his first full-length book. His website is https://www.kenletko.com/.

Flowstone Press

Flowstone Press, an imprint of Left Fork, publishes contemporary poetry collections and chapbooks. Our tastes are eclectic, but we'll lean toward the lyrical, psychological, environmental, cultural, and imagistic.

To learn more about Flowstone, to view our guidelines for submission, or to purchase one or more of our books, please visit **LeftForkBooks.com/Flowstone**

www.ingramcontent.com/pod-product-compliance
Lightning Source LLC
Chambersburg PA
CBHW062031120526
44592CB00037B/2203